TOMATOES BEVERLY

Tomatoes Beverly

Alix Perry

QUERENCIA

Querencia Press – Chicago IL

QUERENCIA PRESS
© Copyright 2025

Alixander Perry

ISBN 978 1 963943 12 2

www.querenciapress.com

First Published in 2025

Querencia Press, LLC
Chicago IL

Printed & Bound in the United States of America

CONTENTS

Preface

Whether drafting prose or poetry, for as long as I can remember I have used music to help keep my brain engaged. The steadily shifting flow of an album or radio show creates a foundation for building a world in words. Around the end of 2022, I started thinking about the subconscious influence my choice of music must have on what I produce. In writing this collection of poems, I set out to explore that effect.

As I worked to create a substantial draft of each poem, I listened exclusively to music by one artist or band. In one case, I ended up combining two poems, hence the naming of that piece after two artists. Only upon returning to the poems to make revisions did I work in silence in order to focus on the finer details. The sole exception to this process is "Interlude," which I purposefully wrote without music.

To be sure, there are recurring themes in these poems. What interested me as this project took shape was the way my ruminations changed in tone and style as my mind engaged with different auditory surroundings. For example, "Insula," written after Moses Sumney, takes a horrific view of the natural world, contrasting sharply with its subdued and meditative characterization in "Magic Dealer," after Big Thief.

The artists and bands after which these poems were written are included to name my appreciation for their inspiration, but also to invite readers to connect with the musical roots of each piece. While these poems can stand alone, and exist together as a collection, I believe presenting them within the context of their creation is all the more illuminating.

Sin Dones
—after Juana Molina

I

Things I should know by now:
whether to take the news with
a grain of salt or a spoonful of sugar;
when to lie and when to brag;
how to celebrate anything at all.

II

Our idols are convincing us not to sleep. Worse, this is the reason
we call them our idols. Teenagers laugh at my 2016 phone when I take
it out to check the forecast. We can't agree on how much rain is too
much. The cabinets don't have enough hot cocoa mix, so I pour
half servings then find out no one likes the mini marshmallows anymore.

III

My singing voice
sounds like
my speaking voice slipping
on a banana peel.
Not panicked
but frictionless.
Don't know how
to stop the tune or
why it started. Breathe
shallow to whisper, deeper
to take blame.
Onerous is the task
of feigned restraint.

Sam, A Dream
—*after Black Belt Eagle Scout*

Our obstinate alabaster duvet
rides a northwesterly wind
into town. The effect is like

a cotton ball: voluminous to the eye,
silent in the ear. The borders so
neatly drawn in color and texture

are temporarily unclear. I am
resisting the urge to chase
ideas without eating breakfast

first. Then I am done resisting.
The tread of my boots is like teeth
into styrofoam. Melts on the tongue.

I scare a rabbit back into
the blackberry bushes.
The flooded fields are frozen

over except where the swans
have broken through. What do you
love the most in this world? What do you

love the least? Is the feeling hate,
indifference, or suppression?
I picture smashed terra cotta

scattered across the highway
intersection. Out of space and time
in the shallow-angled light, I think,

before I realize the color came
to me from the breast of a robin.
The underbelly of winter is warmer

than I remembered. I want to offer
it something. My ideas feel extreme
and I fear they are not enough.

Triple Dog Dare
—after Lucy Dacus

Crossing Butte and 2nd on Saturday
      afternoon, you'll come upon our
finger painted miniatures: not the stuff
      of fantasy games, but cheese boards
and house cats and two-pack toothpaste.
      The domestic necessities, according
to us. Besides practiced dexterity,
      our secret is using an extra-long
pinky nail for the final refinement.
      We sell our work with complimentary
shots of green tea. There are days
      when we are tempted to open a café.
There are days when we ruin the brew
      and offer it with many words of caution.
Our regulars mind their manners and
      shrink their sips. Depending on the
season, the chill of the evening or
      the swarming of its bugs chases us
back to the truck. The windows stay
      rolled down even in winter because
the hand cranks are broken. Repair
      would bring new comforts and ruin
old ones. We bundle up and blast
      the heat while yelling out what we

want for dinner. Our dishes are
      nonsensical inventions meant
to trick the ears: ginger ale
      seashell salad, grilled monsteroni
and cream, tomatoes beverly.
      We compare notes in the driveway
and explain our fantastical dishes
      as if they are well-known delicacies.
And so on we will continue until
      the engine gives out and we sell
the truck for scrap like we've agreed
      and we get rides from friends
whose car windows keep us warm.

Everyone's ████
—*after Surya Botofasina*

The sky eats the sea for breakfast,
the sea, the sky for dinner. The wide

right eye of a storm out of family lore.
Gears forfeiting baby teeth among

flowerbed hailstones. Bolts, their
unspooled threads. Fear is how

the past keeps in touch. A message
of cerebral chemicals like a postcard

from the Oregon Dunes—adorning
my desk decades later. It doesn't

feel so long ago, my palms
salt-stained daily by seashells

and tide stones. My ears stuffed
with teddy bear guts when I didn't

want to listen. Silence, the sound
of dancing blood. We weren't us

then. Now? Three colors of
carpet to cover the living room.

The dish drying rack, glued to
the counter, drains in the wrong

direction. Beside the bathroom mirrors,
I drape red rust-scented curtains.

Like the tack of a clotting cut.
Instincts treading in the sharpest

of places. Conditions of aftermath,
tenuous. I want you to close your

fist around me the same way
you forget: unaware of what's

happening inside your own body.
I'll count backwards from the static

end of the tape and sway out of
time with the floorboards' rattling.

Play Money
—after The New Pornographers

To know the beauty of a boomtown

is to drink from its bottlenecks.
The curation of pleasure, oh

sir/ma'am/etc, you have come

to the right place. To enrich the flows,
their inevitable entanglements.

To distill your economic essence.

Something with which to scent
your bathwater and salt your meat.

A body begins to recognize

itself in its surroundings. Not long,
not long at all. Call it nostalgia or

narcissism, the effect is the same.

In boomtown, the streets paint
themselves with trumpet sounds.

The coffee learns to swallow

infinity, spit it out come morning.
Gossip spreads itself wide and

thick, caviar on a cracker. New

work/life suits incoming this week,
a weave that bends light, sets (y)our

shadow lose to do (y)our bidding.

Cloudy Shoes
—after Damien Jurado

In childhood, I breathed secrets out
my bedroom window. Curious to watch
where they went. Fearful a flashlight
would draw them back like moths.

A movie's protagonist said gravity is
the weight of all the stories we don't know
how to tell. I wore a mosquito net over my
head to protect my windpipe from the shame
of strangers: what I imagined was using
all the bubble bath at once or throwing
spaghetti in front of company.

When I told the cumulus tower clouds ███████
███████, I learned there was a limit to
what the air would take. It started raining. The drops
blew in through the window, an unwelcome echo.

In sickness and in stealth, in equations and
in spells. Those motion machine hands hoping
to hold up a reverberant sky. The visibility was
low that summer. I didn't ask what it meant.

Icebergs
—after Dry Cleaning

If the circumstances
were so dire, I would try
to look busy
cutting a hole in the sky
or dancing a waltz
in 3/0 time. I would put
my face on backwards
to show I'm not
self-conscious like that.

Fortunately for me, rambling
makes for forgiving
kindling. The thought
goes down like
something a snake would feed
its trainer: alive and persistent.

What's this rage
that's been all the rage
lately anyway?

Wait, wait, don't
tell me. It's never as fun
as I expect—
transforming a mystery
into a burden.

I'm trying this new thing
where I spend
too much on groceries.
Word on the street
says it's called
surviving.
Word on the street

is a dying art, no
money in it. No money,
just fortunes.
The man at
the bus stop warns
me not to stick my hand
in the cookie jar,
holds up the nubs of
two fingers and laughs.

Zoo Eyes
—after Aldous Harding

Like a pencil held between two fists, I break
the news. The news is splinters
on the floor. The splinters are
a yellow that went looking

for good fortune and came
back with an aphorism: the eager
cook salts her soils. A broom in one
hand, I drink my meager midnight suspension.

Against the windows, the wind knocks with
a questionable tension. I offer
my guests a jar of pickled
plums as soon as

the first deed is done.
Together we'll confess to
the vultures with the correct sour
scent on our lips. I have three voices to choose

from: one for the fruits of labor, one for the spoils
of war, one for the rot which unites them.
The ground is wet under my
back, though the grass

is dry. My friends are
asking after me. They collect
one-word answers. I laugh to scare off
the consequences and the consequences laugh back.

Prism
—*after Say She She*

Express yourself! They say   I should.

Some celebrations

            are quiet: a room

for tossing my belt   on the floor, for

      letting my hips take   a crack at the ol' job.

Feeling them wonder   about the lower

          bounds of success. By now, most

of the friction must   be muscle memory.

Winded raindrops kaleidoscope   my image,

      seventeen sets of eyelids   closing.

A passing glance   sliced   sideways.

It's all coming back   to me: the reasons

I had for   falling asleep at the kitchen

         counter, nuzzling   the knife block.

There's still something   crude in

    the way   I choose my words.

Too many gas   can characters populating

the life I knew. My   steps   regretting

themselves across   the concrete. My my my.

To what do I owe   this great honor?

And again. Questions   bitten down

to the quick. I'm not   supposed to keep

my lights on too late. Because   what

if I lose it? The instinct   for sleep,

the surrender   of onward.

Don't Let it Get to You(r Head)
—after Andy Shauf

You say it's flooding in a faraway place called home.
And the days are getting longer.

                              Don't let it get to your
head, like you've done something to deserve the light.

Filtered as it may be through thick clouds. Tempt me
with a spare story. And I will try to set

                              the record for
a phone call's longest pause—sighing loudly so you

know the connection hasn't dropped—before asking if
if you mean Suspenders Mark or Mark With

                              the Loud Dog.
But it's Pasta Salad Mark, who I didn't realize was back

in town. After his divorce, maybe I should have guessed.
He used to muse across

                         the breakroom table about
meeting someone who would show him a new side of life.

It's unoriginal to poke fun at idealists, so I'll watch
my tone as I ask if his

                              pasta salad business has gone
under yet. You'll tell me I need to cut it out with those

  questions that imply a single answer. Stringing the line
  with stronger bait, I'll wonder

                              aloud if Mark might
ever sell the rights to his recipes, knowing you'll go

                                          forth satirizing a plan for pasta salad empire.

Insula

—after Moses Sumney

The layers go
like this:
hot rock,
colder rock,
bedrock,
remnants of death
and life,
life
and death,
recent death and
current life.
My steps used
to land with an echo,
and
I did not
understand why.
Water is a tool
of distance.
The dead sink
then float
then
sink again. Mercy.

The body
exhales
its final air,
and the
vacuum is nothing
but an
instant.
No space.
The echo. Did not understand.
Why?
The catch of the day
is unidentifiable.
It doesn't make
the menu.
We nibble
buttered noodles
and sip
age-appropriate drinks.
We have lost track
of our ages
but assume
we are young.

What else would we be? The
young
do not understand.
The naive.
The echo.
I spit my wounds
up and out,
nowhere
but the brink,
nothing
but sedition.
I am my own namesake,
you know?
The layers go
imprecisely
like this:
growth,
undergrowth,
decay,
absence,
decay,
profit,

decay,
doubt,
bedrock,
harder rock,
hotter rock. The
point of no return.
I sound like a
trip-
ty-
ch
walking the plank.
The reckless imagination

makes
the criminal.
My steps used
to land with an echo.
I think I understand
why. The earth is porous—in
ways
we understand,
in ways
we do not.
The possibilities live
inside

the impossibilities,
their
terrestrial burrows.
My steps used
to land   land   land   land.
All that is buried
seeks a life
in our bones.
What else
would
we be?

Interlude

The horizon holds confessions
no one wants to hear,
so it speaks them through

the fingers of last light while
I fall asleep under

the weight of ordinary fibers,
paying the cost of a street
legal bleeding, my skin smile

of tiny incisors. It's mostly nights
I succumb to that old

bag of tricks: frost
chiseling gravel's words,
dearth of my reflection in

a river gone brown,
dusk mutiny of the minutes.

Condolences to the daffodils
shaking in their boots.
I wouldn't want to risk a late

bloom either. The image returns, not
infrequently: those yellow

heads limp in the citied
slush. Patience, dear patience, tell us
of sharp & tell us of song.

Be Careful With Yourself
—after Julia Jacklin

The coast resembles more
a jawline each day. Too sharp,

it wants for much, I think,
misses the predictable

violences. Hours inland,
my (con)temporary home

holds a faint tidal rhythm. I play
percussion against the walls,

lose the beat quickly. Distance
imposes its limits on synchronicity.

Time an unkind relative,
a begrudging out-of-stepparent.

I don't trust my mind to dwell
here responsibly. I hire

hecklers to tell me the good news.
I take notes, read up. If nothing else,

my solace is well-researched. I've found,
for example, that suddenly shifTING TO

CAPS LOCK IS LIKELY to coax the poet
to smile to themself. Call it soliloquized

science. Grant it equal standing with
the fantasies of ████████ that soak

my shins in brine and silt. What washes off
easily gives credit where credit is taboo.

Tonight, we're imbibing on azure in the key
of G. My name is on the list, and they wrap

my wrist with a green fabric band. The sun
is a match head in the sky. Rainbows

marble the ground. A professional
drummer accompanies the singer,

and my finger tapping becomes
inconsequential. I decide

there is no lost time, only moments
we're no longer bearing. The wind

is dying down; the hour
is nigh for the flyer to land

her sea cucumber kite. The water
is retreating with all the momentum

of bad stagefright. I slip from the crowd
and walk to the break, convinced

I obey gravity by choice. The rocks slosh
with ripples, suggestions from the fount.

It's just a draining bathtub's gurgle,
a breath that bows the surface.

Red Eyes
—*after The War on Drugs*

I doubt I'll ever cook like
the legend of the costco

chicken pot pie. Growing
up, served any way I liked it,

on flimsy paper plates one
week, fine china the next.

You would eat yours scooped
into that heavy orange mug with

the chipped handle and the
stencil of a single acorn.

I hated your habit of talking with
your mouth full, but instead of

stopping, you convinced me to
begin. In the end, there still wasn't

enough time to hear all I wanted
you to say. This first summer alone,

my neighbors spray paint
their brown grass green.

The service takes a gradual route
to perfection, a shade darker

on each night's visit, two weeks
in total. They ignore the crests

and depressions in the land,
the routes where groundwater

would trace a gradient with its
run and pool. Vanishing topography,

like when you took the couch and
I took the bed and the cleaners

shampooed flat our pockmarked carpet.
A borrowed space for our borrowed

time. Yet rivers still run red in
my memory of your eyes,

carving canyons toward iris blue.

Hypochondriac
—after Fenne Lily

My thoughts go bump
in the night like a giant
running a marathon.
Backtracking through
overfull fields of divine
sentiment. The tickle of
the borage is a misplaced
wink. In the cold, the cold,
rubbing a calf against
a shin, that fleeting heat,
the promises I used to make.

Clouds ten by gracious ten,
consuming plumes of ivory.
I wanted you to see my sorrow
before it was bound and sold.
Too late, too late. We feel always
too late because we do not
know for what we are early.

I'd say I'm getting better, on
general trend. Underpasses
beg their rain shadows into
place and puddles rust
themselves red. Days go
wrong, go right, go rogue.
It's a direct address, the way
I speak to the spectacle,
the river ripple-torn. Picture
my words descending
the nearest eddy, caught
for a season, maybe longer.

Ídolo

—*after Adrian Quesada*

Critics are calling it forty
minutes of your life you'll never
get back. It's the new new-wave,
our sonic masquerade.
A velvety entropy of side-mouthed
smiles. Helpful on those days
spent searching for
the perfect staircase upon which
to act out a downward spiral.

Critics are calling it a trivial
embellishment of breath.
The body the central problem,
its proclivity to open.
In winter's cold you can sometimes
see ghosts giving life to air.
A jubilee of inefficiency.

Critics are calling
premonition an art
and recollection a science.
Like how every raindrop has
a signature shadow:
reproducible delicacies
for the shop down
the street. They taste of
coconut and clover,
or so I am told. But it's
really the texture—
presence and absence—
that draws the crowds.
Let the record show
I watch my back like
I watch my mouth: longingly.

Pitch or Honey
—after Neko Case

I work hard, become a real crier's crier.
I play classic static on my gramophone,
my sustained refrain, pitter patter of
imagined witches. Though I come from

analogue superstition, I want to break
bread with the changing times. New
victim of sonic vanity, recording

the sound of each sunset in hope of
seizing truth. The dedication comes
and goes like a fever, latches and

burrows like a curse. I make a plan
to settle down inside a bearable
scene: where the river bends, where

the rocks paint pretty with habitual water,
where soles are as much silt as skin.
And a whistle let loose always circles
back, comes home. Come home.

Natural Information
—*after Bill Callahan*

Dusky hues, fat enough
to pinch between
fingers, I think to
count the shades
between purple and
pink and give up before
I begin. My personal
first rate minutiae
for this idle eve.
Playing pareidolia
with the burls on
the ancient cherry
tree. Shadowing
soft-edged puppets
of knuckle and nail.
I've been learning to
ask myself for everything
I think I deserve.
The alders reach their
branches higher
with each yawn.

So Long
—*after Danielle Ponder*

- The rush of sediment that browns the delta
- The seabed where it settles
- The boots that wade you through your wrongs
- The heater that wafts them dry
- The salt that scrubs out secrets
    - some easier than others
- The ceiling with its ineloquent apology
- The pretty thought of an ugly time
    - in feat if not in fashion
- The tears that answer to a mail-order logic
- The invitation that elides excuse
- The neon that glazes the eyes
    - the pairs
    - and pairs
    - and all the pairs
- The glossed cans that break once to open and once to collapse
- The pour that ambers the bathroom sink
- The discards that decorate the ditches
- The blanched hands that fill linted pockets
    - scraping a way to warmth

When the Lights Go / Against Your Mind
—after Totally Enormous Extinct Dinosaurs / Built to Spill

So, you want to witness power.
　　　　What do you want me to do about it?
I'm not up to much in my leased

　　　　300 square feet, on my walks to
the saddest supermarket in town,
　　　　the one with the red floppy tube air

guy thing like a strip mall's used
　　　　car mart. They say the owner's uncle
once nursed dreams of running a candy

　　　　shop out of what used to be a
banking drive thru. But the uncle's
　　　　dead now or maybe just moved

away. Regardless, the bulk gummies
　　　　are always going stale these days.
I have my own dreams too, you know?

　　　　To nail my winter oranges to the ceiling,
one by one, ward off every ghost. To sit
　　　　still for enough hours to watch the trees

massage shadow into light and light back
        into shadow. And, on the snowy days,
assuming they come this year like

        last, to hear a few branches breaking
for lunch: snap, snap, munch. You
        want to witness power, probably

something about the oneness of creation
        and destruction? Sometimes our days are
much ~~less~~ more than exciting. I'm tossing

        the neighborhood possums a handful
of wrinkled marshmallows this evening,
        booting puddles in the dusk-empty park.

Comes a Day
—after Built to Spill

There's this free clinic by the rickshaw
station, downtown, you know, at the
intersection of the iceberg and tornado
alleys. The receptionist hands you
a lollipop and a sticker to congratulate
you for getting this far.

> You have been spending the days whittling
> the ends of sticks sharper and your body hurts
> all over. When you asked why they needed
> so many sharp sticks, they said you had
> a great talent. Before bed, you scrub under
> your nails even though you never see anything
> stuck there, only feel it.

The doctor takes 25 scans to locate
the problem(s). She says some
of the past lives in your blood, some
in your marrow. All your mind has
tried to excise. Her suggestions include
simulated good times and marrying into
better insurance.

> The sparkly turtle sticker is a scratch
> and sniff that smells of cigarette smoke:
> a kitschy nicotine patch. The lollipop,
> a pill splitter. Its puny blade wouldn't
> whittle for long. You wonder what
> you'll sharpen when they run
> out of wood. Inside your purse,
> copies of the x-rays are still warm.

Go, Stay
—after L'Rain

Winds blow serpentine life
into blackberry tendrils draping
alder branches, sawdust aching
humid below. April's faint

impression of warmth, like
hummingbird tracks in sand.
In the right light, with the right
attitude, you might document

the evidence. Either way, time
will show itself eventually. Green-
gold fists of fruit. Lesser peaks
losing track of their white hats.

Downhill lurks the city, polished
by its noise, defiant in its rhythms.
Where 9-5ers prestige their steps
with clockwork heels. Such a mass

of metal and glass, gravity that
invents orbits and quells escapes.
Gives what you want, takes what
you need before you know you

need it. The wind gusts again, and
I admit my second layer too thin.
I give the skyline a view of my back,
dare its mass to come and get me.

Don't Swallow the Cap
—after The National

One day, I'll have a tattoo on
      the back of my thumb that says
remember to floss. I'll be practical
      like that, and easily motivated

by guilt. I won't be in touch with
      C anymore, and I'll use his gifted
english lavender to mark
      the springs since we've spoken.

I'll go alone to places I was
      taught to go with others. To play
phone tetris and eavesdrop
      on drunken drama. To ~~dance~~ trip

my feet in the stage's shadow.
      I'll catch my fall in the rare summer
mud, rub my fingerprints out with
      a knuckle. I'll change my mind and

sign my initials, an autograph for
      the witnesses. The singer will surprise
me, having gone gray. I won't have
      noticed in his pictures: these tricks of

the light just our eyes primed
        for comfort. I'll want to ask him
when his youth ran out. As if it
        happens the way a fridge falls

empty. I'll think of my old dentist saying
        my teeth were aging faster than the rest
of my body. I'll look down at my thumb,
        imagine those blood cells nibbling ink.

Magic Dealer
—after Big Thief

How the earth scrapes the sky

to carve a line for our stories. While flick-whip

winds polish arches and

heap dunes. Never one without the other,

that howl between

them still lonelies. The color of longing,

chamomile street lamps

steeping in fog. How it weighs weightlessly,

the arrogant night,

a wall walked into but never through. Each

puffed sound muffled

into false distance. Await, aright, afoot, apiece.

The next stroke

upon our malleable body. The last flood

through the wash

until the dust begs for comfort and you open

your window to listen.

Desandar
—after Boogarins

It was the sticky surface of the floodplain
that raised us. Have you ever seen a sapling
so verdant that the rain stains the ground green

at its base? Arborous mess like a felt pen burst
at the bottom of a backpack. Spreading fast.

Quickly. Quickening. Fastening myself to
something stable. Or trying. Under a wide enough

scope, everything gyring. We were newly eight
and ringed by party store tiki torches when
we looked up at the stars and claimed to feel

the Earth turning. High on the first night of
summer. Kick the can, dogs the finders'

unfair allies. Noses rustling leaves, feet
snapping twigs, the neighbor's distant shotgun.

We hid in twos or threes and forgot to turn off
our flashlights. We whispered about cougars and
coyotes. Screamed because it was so much to

feel at once. The mysteries quit asking
permission at sundown. Deeper into the

woods, pushing toward a property line
that never proved itself real enough to find.

Acknowledgements

First, thank you to the editors of the following publications for providing some of the poems in this collection with their first homes:

many wor(l)ds: "Zoo Eyes"
FERAL: "When the Lights Go / Against Your Mind"
Papers Publishing: "Sin Dones," "Sam, A Dream," and "Don't Swallow the Cap"
Squawk Back: "Play Money" and "Desandar"
Lammergeier: "Everyone's ███████" as "Everyone's [Redacted]"

Mountains of gratitude to the artists who created the music that inspired this collection. I am also so appreciative of Querencia Press for sharing in my vision and publishing this collection. Thank you to my friends and my family for their support. And, to the KEXP crew, thank you for your unending enthusiasm and warmth. You inspire my inner fan to dance on the back of my inner critic.

www.ingramcontent.com/pod-product-compliance
Lightning Source LLC
Chambersburg PA
CBHW081725120626

46550CB00010B/3254